PHILMONT WHERE SPIRITS SOAR

Copyright © 1989

Boy Scouts of America
Irving, Texas

FIRST EDITION

ISBN 0-8395-4079-5
No. 4079

Library of Congress Catalog Number 89-081760

Manufactured in United States of America

Silver on the sage, starlit skies above,

Aspen covered hills, country that I love.

Philmont, here's to thee, Scouting paradise,

Out in God's country—tonight.

Wind in whispering pines, eagles soaring high,

Purple mountains rise, against an azure sky.

Philmont, here's to thee, Scouting paradise,

Out in God's country—tonight.

▲▲

Philmont Hymn

PHILMONT WHERE SPIRITS SOAR

Jerry Poppenhouse	*Project director, photographer and photo editor*
Joe Williams	*Writer*
Jim Knight, Kerry Walsh	*Designers*
Thad Allton, Cecelia Cox,	*Photographers*
Mark Groth, David Halpern,	
Kurt Maurer, Lisa Means,	
Daniel Overturf	
Larry Walker	*Logistics and photographer*
Susan Gray	*Production*
Nancy Caffoe, Lisa Moyer	*Proofing, editing*
Rodgers Lithographing Co.	*Printing*
Unigraph	*Color separations*
Roswell	*Bookbinding*

//////////

For more than 50 years, the Tooth of Time has held
a special place in the hearts and minds of more than
500,000 Scouts who have experienced the magic,
the wonder that is Philmont.

Foreward

The Phillips family has long been associated with the Boy Scouts. Waite Phillips, oil entrepreneur, donated the New Mexico land that is now Philmont Scout Ranch, along with the PhilTower office building in Tulsa, Oklahoma, to help finance the Ranch's operations. Phil Phillips, son of the cofounder of Phillips Petroleum Company, has been a longtime supporter of the Boy Scouts, and served as president of a Scout council for 20 years.

So, it was fitting that many years ago Phillips Petroleum joined the Phillips family in support of the Boy Scouts. Phillips employees have served Scouting in local, regional, and national offices. The Phillips Petroleum Foundation has provided financial backing to many Scouting programs.

Now, Phillips proudly assists in bringing to Scouting this book about the rustic beauty and character-building activities at Philmont Scout Ranch. We hope this book will bring back the spirit of adventure of Philmont to the people who have been there, and help inspire them, and others, to use their time and talents for the continuing success of the Boy Scout movement.

Glenn A. Cox
President and Chief Operating Officer
Phillips Petroleum Company

"Some think that happiness

comes from getting, others know

that it comes from giving."

▲▲

Sir Robert S.S. Baden-Powell.

He founded the Boy Scouts

in 1908 to develop citizenship,

character, self-reliance,

and helpfulness to others.

Introduction

The Spirit of Philmont

Philmont is a feeling, a wilderness, a challenge, a fellowship, a quality of light, a grand adventure, a magical experience, a memory, a spirit.

Philmont is the craggy, beckoning, million-year-old Sangre de Cristo Mountains, with rain and lightning in the afternoons, hiking trails that go up and never seem to come down, cotton-woods, willows, ponderosa pines and aspens, black bears, elk, coyotes and cougars, Indian paintbrush and Rocky Mountain iris, and eagles, hawks and ravens soaring high in the crisp, azure sky.

Each summer, Philmont initiates some 16,000 Scouts—boys and girls alike—from the Bronx to Bakersfield, from Tokyo to Tupelo, from ages 13 to 17, urban and rural, confident and scared. They come to these 214 square miles in northeastern New Mexico for high adventure and they get it in big doses. Leaving behind the world of Big Macs and MTV they shoulder a 35-pound pack and spend 12 days hiking 50, sometimes even 100, miles through awe-inspiring mountains and valleys. On their trek, they learn how to tie a fly, ride a horse, pan for gold, climb a rock wall, fish for trout, shoot a .30-06 Springfield rifle, and survive in the rugged backcountry.

Thanks to a seasonal staff of more than 600 dedicated young adults who seem much older and wiser than their years, Philmont's 137,493 acres are amazingly unmarked by this summer intrusion of youth. The Scouts are not. Most of them leave changed, affected by the powerful, magnetic pull of these mountains and the solitude of the clear night air. They go home with the usual blisters and sore muscles and hurry to chuck their MoGos and pemican bars for fast food and an ice-cold soda. They take with them memories of overcoming physical and mental barriers thrown in their path by the mountains, the weather, and each other. But when all is said and done, they leave Philmont with more than memories—they leave with a respect and responsibility for this fragile land. They leave with an awareness of their own inner spirit and all that goes with it: fragility, energy, self-esteem, confidence, cooperation, growth, and peace.

This book is about the spirit of Philmont. It is a story about the benevolence of Waite Phillips, who gave the Boy Scouts of America

Like riders on the silver sage, Philmont Scouts see the world
from a higher dimension.

the land and the vision to make it possible. It is a story about those who have nurtured this land over the last 50 years and kept the dream alive. It is a story about the 500,000 Scouts who have gone through Philmont and the Scout leaders who continue to bring them to these magical mountains. And in particular, it is a story of the young men and women who work as seasonal staff members at Philmont each summer—returning time and again to savor the feeling, the giving, the scenery, the atmosphere, the family that is Philmont. They keep the Philmont experience alive; they are the spirit of Philmont.

At Fish Camp, Scouts learn to tie a fly —and test their skills fishing for trout.

Scouts in Philmont's Cavalcades program straddle the saddle for eight days, exploring the backcountry like the mountain men of old. Here, at Beaubien Camp, they relax after a day on the range.

The sheer numbers make you think the worst: 14,000 Scouts tromping through 137,493 acres of land in a 68-day period. On the surface, it looks like the environment would suffer tremendously from this summer onslaught of campers.

It probably would if it were in hands other than the Boy Scouts of America. The Scouting organization at Philmont has the use of the land down to a science. They know that the land is impacted, but they do their best to make it low-impact.

The Philmont conservation program makes an impact on the Scouts themselves. Every Scout at Philmont is taught about low-impact camping and how to care for the land. Each Scout signs a wilderness pledge and spends three hours doing conservation work. Throughout their time at Philmont, the terms "low-impact, no-trace camping" are ingrained in them so when they leave, they take the ability and desire to practice this wilderness ethic back home or anywhere else they might camp.

"Conservation is selfish—it's for man," says John Deal, a 25-year-old seasonal staffer who is in his ninth season at Philmont. "The whole reason we want to save this Philmont resource is for those who come after us. The rocks don't care, the deer aren't smart enough to care, the bears would rather have us gone, I think. It's for us. That's the whole reason for conservation. The land is what's between us, it's what binds us together."

▲▲

Conservation

Philmont's Sangre de Cristo Mountains rise from the New Mexico plains, giving Scouts their first view of the southern edge of the Rocky Mountains.

Those who complete their Philmont trek and have donated three hours of conservation work receive the coveted Arrowhead Patch.

*Philmont is home on the range where
the deer and the antelope play, and the Scouts
have room to roam.*

A 1,100-pound elk with an antler spread of more than five feet waits around the next bend in the trail at Philmont.

How often do teenagers have the opportunity to come eye-to-eye with a great horned owl?

*For 50 years, Inspiration Point has enveloped its
visitors in its majesty, causing the most boisterous
to suddenly turn pensive.*

Sunset
The clouds were slowly moving
They looked like drifts of snow
But were soon changing
Into a crimson glow.

I watched them slowly disappear
And felt a sadness in my heart
But then I heard a small voice say
There will be another day.

There will be more sunsets
Very beautiful to see
It is God's gift to everyone
And all of them are free.

Esther Poppenhouse

Waite Phillips gave the Boy Scouts of America the idea, the land, and the funds for Philmont. Worth almost $40 million, he started with nothing and made his fortune in the pell-mell oil play of the 1920s. "His every waking moment was spent putting effort into doing something," says his son, Elliot "Chope" Phillips, a New Mexico rancher.

Chapter One

The Roots of Philmont:
Waite Phillips

Waite Phillips left the party inside Villa Philmonte and stood on the porch of his rambling Spanish-Mediterranean summer home outside Cimarron, New Mexico. He gazed across the wide expanse of lawn, across the pasture where his buffalo grazed freely, all the way to where the land gave way to the Rocky Mountains. In the distance he could see Window Rock and Cathedral Rock peaks. He owned it all: the mountains before him, the plains to the south. Altogether it amounted to almost 300,000 acres of prime ranch land and rugged mountains that spired 13,000 feet. The year was 1938. He was 55 years old. And he was thinking about giving a big chunk of this land away.

Waite wished his twin brother, Wiate, were still alive to be part of all this. It seemed like only yesterday they were adventurous 16-year-olds leaving their poor but beloved Creston, Iowa, to see the world. For two years they traveled and worked odd jobs—as Western Union boys, dishwashers, laborers, kitchen help, farmers, and ranch hands. In the Bitterroot Mountains of Montana they built a log cabin and tested their mettle through the winter by trapping animals and living off the land.

But in Spokane, tragedy struck: Wiate died of a ruptured appendix. Waite remembered the sadness he felt when he took his brother's body home to Iowa on the train. Devastated by the loss, he stayed close to home for the next few years, first attending business school and later working as a bookkeeper for a coal company in Knoxville, Iowa. There his spirits were lifted when he fell in love and married Genevieve Elliot.

Waite's two older brothers, Frank and L.E., had left Iowa for Indian Territory to make their mark in banking and oil. They would eventually form a company called Phillips Petroleum in Bartlesville, Oklahoma.

In 1906, Waite joined his older brothers, and spent eight years in the booming oil fields becoming their field superintendent. Frank taught his young brother how to be a businessman. He learned fast and he learned it all and became a top-notch operator. Though he had immense respect for Frank, the driving force behind Phillips Petroleum, Waite wanted to head up his own firm, to be his own man. In 1916, he left Phillips Petroleum and went into the oil business for himself. He formed the Waite Phillips Oil Company and struck it rich immediately.

Waite positioned his company as one of the first oil firms to enter almost every aspect of the oil business: exploration, marketing, leasing, and transportation. His strategy paid off handsomely, for in 1918 it was said he was making $30,000 a day from his oil wells. For the next six years, Waite Phillips went on a run, buying oil leases by the score and hitting more winners than losers. In 1925 he sold his company for $25 million in cash. He was 44 years old and worth almost $40 million personally. When asked the key to his success, he said, "It was luck."

With more money than some nations even had at the time, Waite invested in stocks and bonds, oil, banks, and real estate. He soon held 500,000 acres of land in Colorado, New Mexico, and Arizona. His prize was his 300,000 acres in the Sangre de Cristo Mountains near Cimarron, New Mexico. It was here that he built his summer home, Villa Philmonte, which was a smaller version of his 72-room Italian-Mediterranean estate in Tulsa called Philbrook. Both mansions were designed by Edward Buehler Delk, who designed the Country Club Plaza shopping center in Kansas City.

Villa Philmonte stands on land steeped in history. It was here that frontier scouts like Kit Carson lived and where Spanish conquistadors searched for the Lost City of Gold. Ancient Indians etched their stories in the canyon walls, and the Santa Fe Trail showed settlers the way west. This area was once part of the stupendous million-acre Maxwell Land Grant, one of the largest pieces of land to be owned by one man in the history of the United States. But now it belonged to Waite Phillips, and here he built one of the best cattle herds in the country. Villa Philmonte played host to visiting dignitaries such as aviator Wiley Post, U. S. Vice President Charles Dawes, author Kenneth L. Roberts, and Oklahoma humorist Will Rogers. Phillips saw that trails were cut into the mountains, and his entourage would ride into the backcountry and hunt and fish to their heart's delight. They would be gone for days, staying at one of his hunting or fishing lodges he had constructed. When they returned they would retire to the splendid luxury of Villa Philmonte.

Over the last few years, he had grown even more restless. The cattle business required patience and Waite Phillips didn't have a lot of patience—he was the type who was always looking for a new horizon, a new challenge. "His every waking moment was spent putting effort into doing something," says his son Chope, a New Mexico rancher. Once he built something up, whether it was an oil company or a ranch, his interests started to turn elsewhere. And now his business interests were turning away from his Philmont Ranch. Yet he fiercely loved this land and mountains and wanted them put to a proper use.

The laughter of the guests inside Villa Philmonte interrupted Waite's thoughts. But it didn't matter. He had already resolved what he had long believed. Under his breath he said, "The only things we keep are those we give away." He took one last glance at his mountains silhouetted in front of the setting sun, then turned and walked into the courtyard and re-joined the party.

The next morning he wrote the Boy Scouts of America to offer them a gift: 35,857 acres of land and $50,000 for its development into a Boy Scout camp. Scout officials were at first reluctant to accept. After all, how could they possibly maintain and operate this land? They were in the Scouting business, not the land business. It took a trip to Philmont to arouse their enthusiasm; the mountains worked their magic, and they accepted. They named it Philturn Rocky Mountain Scoutcamp, playing off the name Phillips and the word "turn" meaning the Good Turn every Scout should do daily. The date was November 22, 1938.

Three years later, Waite Phillips gave the Boy Scouts 91,358 more acres of land, Villa Philmonte, and his magnificent 23-story Phil-tower office building in Tulsa, the rent proceeds of which would help offset operating costs of the Scout camp. An elated group of Scout executives marveled at their prize. It was renamed Philmont Scout Ranch.

Waite Phillips said he hoped his gift would "inspire and train boys in the virtues of faith, initiative, self-reliance, resourcefulness, and courage."

Throughout his life Waite Phillips always gave credit for his immense financial success to nothing more than luck. But when a Scout from Indiana who has never seen the mountains, never caught a rainbow trout, never slept 10,000 feet high under the stars comes to Philmont, that is surely the kind of luck Waite Phillips had in mind when he gave the land to the Boy Scouts.

Waite Phillips went on to dabble in Los Angeles real estate. He returned to his beloved Philmont time and again over the next 26 years. Often he would ride his horse to the backcountry and visit with Scouts, usually keeping his identity a secret. But today, on his last trip to Philmont, he would stay in the distance and simply watch and listen and reflect on so many things, but especially on his gift and how by giving it away it would go on giving to others long after he was gone.

Change was in the wind and the world would never be the same again. But there would always be Philmont and the mountains and the Scouts, and Waite Phillips would know and understand. He would always know.

One of the earliest photos of the Phillips brothers.
From left: Ed, Waite, Fred, Frank, and L.E.

Businessman and benefactor,
Waite Phillips had the foresight to
envision the future, a future built
around a place called Philmont.

The Phillips brothers: too much alike when it came to business. From the left: Fred, Waite, Ed, L.E., Frank.

Villa Philmonte, the summer home of Waite and Genevieve Phillips, was patterned after their 72-room Italian-Mediterranean estate in Tulsa. Built in 1927, it hosted guests such as U.S. Vice President Charles Dawes and Oklahoma humorist Will Rogers.

Today, Villa Philmonte is open for tours to Scouts and the public. Additional buildings were constructed on the grounds and serve as the Philmont Training Center headquarters, the leading site for adult Scout leader training programs and conferences.

The Philmont cattle brand.

Philmont was a cattle ranch before it was a Scout ranch. Today, it is both, with 220 cows, 200 calves, 80 heifers, 15 bulls, 200 horses, 135 buffalo, 18,000 Scouts, and three full-time cowboys.

Elbert Fretwell (left), Chief Scout Executive, visits with Waite Phillips (center), and Walter Head, president of the Boy Scouts in 1940.

Originally called Philturn Rocky Mountain Scout-camp, Philmont used this patch through 1941.

My dad had a real love for Philmont. He was a very complex person. He was serious but warm, compassionate but ambitious, and generous to a fault. He was a great reader, an excellent negotiator, and had little patience for anything short of perfection. He was the kind of man who was always looking for something new, always striving for perfection. Every waking minute of his life was spent putting effort into doing something. That's why he never stayed with one thing very long— he got bored easily.

Dad's brother, Frank, started Phillips Petroleum Company and stayed with it all his life. My dad sold his oil company just as it was going good. I always thought he should have stayed in the oil business because it was fast-moving and changing and that was Dad's nature. Dad had a real love for the land that is now Philmont, but he never had much patience when it came to ranching.

Ever since I was a kid, I never wanted to be anything else but a rancher, to stay here on the land. In that respect I was like my mother. I always knew where my place was in this world— it was on the land. But Dad never understood that about me. He wanted me to be a businessman.

I was 23 years old when Dad gave the Boy Scouts the land for Philmont. I think he really thought he was doing me a favor by giving it away, like it would keep me from becoming a rancher. But how I wish I would have inherited this land—not so much the part that he gave the Scouts, I think what he did for them was marvelous, but he sold off a lot of surrounding ranch land to others at that time and he sold it dirt-cheap, he just about gave it away.

ELLIOT "CHOPE" PHILLIPS, SON OF WAITE PHILLIPS. HE IS 71 YEARS OLD AND OPERATES A RANCH NEAR WATROUS, NEW MEXICO. FOR MANY YEARS HE SERVED ON THE PHILMONT RANCH COMMITTEE. HE HAS BEEN A RANCHER ALL HIS LIFE.

Some things never change: Scouts in 1940 knew that the chuck wagon meant one thing: food!

The outdoors has always been the focus of the Scouting program. Around the camp-fire, these early-day Scouts learn about Indian lore.

Ranching

*Before Philmont was a Scout ranch, it was a cattle
ranch. And it continues today as a working operation,
complete with some 220 cows, 200 calves,
80 heifers, 200 horses, 135 buffalo, a smattering
of burros, and three full-time, real-life cowboys:
Bob Ricklefs, Ben Vargas, and Rod Taylor .*

*The ranch horses are also used in two Philmont Scout
programs: at three of the backcountry camps
for short trail rides led by seasonal staff members,
and in the Cavalcades, a rugged eight-day
horseback pack trip through the mountains in the
style of trappers and mountain men. In these, crews
of 10 to 12 Scouts experience the full range of thrills,
from saddle sores to caring for a horse on the trail,
and from panoramic vistas to a feeling of oneness
with their horse and with nature.*

*The way of the cowboy hasn't changed much at Philmont.
Cattle must still be driven to the high country.*

Bob Ricklefs first came to Philmont as a Scout. He has been the ranch superintendent for 17 years.

Bob Ricklefs, ranch superintendent, says, "We have water

rights that most people in New Mexico would die for, and it alone

is one of the greatest gifts that Waite Phillips left us.

We irrigate maybe 250 acres and cut hay to supplement our grazing

needs. In all, we probably use 250 tons of hay a year."

Head 'em up, move 'em out!
Roundup time!

Rod Taylor, one of Philmont's three full-time cowboys, pauses to reflect on the day at the bunkhouse in the high country.

This elk's roof was snowed on.

Teenage Scouts today aren't easily buffaloed. Like the American bison, Scouts at Philmont learn what it takes to survive in the wilderness. The real application comes when they return home to apply their newly found skills in their everyday lives.

*Learning to cope with the elements is a major part
of the Scouts' training at Philmont. Storm clouds like
these mean they are in for another on-the-spot test.*

"At the end of the open road

we come to ourselves."

—Louis Simpson

Chapter Two

Welcome to Philmont!

Twenty wide-eyed Scouts pop out of the dusty, bug-splattered bus like popcorn from a popper. They stretch off the confinement of a 24-hour trip from Texas, and are met by an enthusiastic "Welcome to Philmont!" from an 18-year-old Ranger. He shakes their hands and looks each one square in the eye and asks: "How was your trip?" "What's your name?" "Have you ever been to Philmont before?" "I like your shirt!" "I can tell, you're gonna love it here!"

I was incredibly tired when I arrived. We somehow managed to turn an 11-hour bus ride into a 24-hour nightmare. I don't know what I expected, but I didn't expect the mountains to be so big. They rose right up out of the plains. The first thing I remember was meeting our Ranger, Ken Block. I was the youngest member of the crew, just 13 at the time. We did so many things the first day—walking around Base Camp, checking out equipment, standing in line. It was a long day. This was the first time I had been completely out of my element . . .

A Scout's introduction to Philmont begins with a Ranger and ends with a Ranger. From the outset, it is the Ranger who sets the tone for a Scout's 12 days of adventure, and it is the Ranger who is responsible for the safety, ethics, values, skills, and attitudes of each crew. A heavy responsibility for 18- to 22-year-old college students. But these young adults shoulder it well. They genuinely care and respect this wilderness and are intensely concerned that the Scouts not only have a great time and learn camping skills, but also learn something about themselves and the land.

"We teach our Rangers the concept of leading from behind," says Paul Kapfer, a recent graduate of Valparaiso University, who is responsible for training Philmont's Rangers. "We teach Rangers to lead through each crew's elected crew leader. It's the Ranger's responsibility to teach safety and camping skills the crew needs but not to be the leader of the trek. We want these 13- to 17-year-old Scouts to find their own potential and to make their own decisions."

That decision-making begins immediately in Base Camp, a holding area, supply base, and command center. In 1988, 18,646 Scouts came through Philmont in only a three-month span. And all went through Base Camp. Up to 3,000 Scouts are in Base Camp each day. Half are arriving; half are departing.

Dave Bates, director of program, is one of 50 permanent full-time BSA staff people at Philmont. Responsible for the Base Camp, backcountry, and trekking programs, he says: "Since 1975, we have had a complete transformation in Base Camp—almost all our buildings have been built since then."

Bates and his staff have this would-be logistical nightmare down to a fine art. Before Scouts ever set foot on Philmont they will have selected one of 24 itineraries ranging in difficulty from typical to super-strenuous. Once at Philmont, this makes it possible for them to arrive one day and hit the trail the next. In that short time each crew meets with their Ranger, checks into the overnight platform tent city, receives group equipment, double-checks their itinerary, takes a crew photo, conducts health rechecks, and eats in the mess hall—the last prepared and served food they will have for two weeks.

Crew leaders—Scouts who are elected by their fellow Scouts—and adult advisers attend orientation meetings, and if there is time, Scouts tour Villa Philmonte, the Seton Memorial Library, or the Kit Carson Museum. At 7:00 in the evening, everything closes for an hour so Scouts can attend a religious service—either Catholic, Jewish, Mormon, or Protestant. Afterwards, those who are just starting their trek attend an opening campfire; those returning from their trek attend a closing campfire where they are awarded their prized Philmont patch and the much sought after "We all made it" patch signifying their accomplishment.

Each crew at Philmont hikes a set itinerary that takes them through backcountry camps where they experience a different program each day, ranging from horseback riding to rock climbing, and from blacksmithing to black powder rifle shooting. They are self-sufficient on the trail, carrying three to four days worth of food with them at a time. Through Philmont's ingenious supply system, backcountry food locations at key places on the trails let Scouts resupply their food.

We hiked over Mount Baldy the second day — that's almost 12,441 feet! I was incredibly tired. Our Ranger cooked cobbler in a cast-iron dutch oven. He told us he carried it in his pack from Base Camp. We believed him; we later found out that it was stored at the campsite. Cypher's Mine in Central Country was the turning point of our trek, where we all came together as a team. Until then we had different people hiking at different speeds. Halfway up the trail our assistant Scoutmaster sat down and said he quit as assistant Scoutmaster of Troop 836. We all had to think, 'Why would Mr. Walker just stop like that?' We finally realized that he was having a hard time climbing, and nobody was thinking about his needs and feelings. From that point on, we hiked as a team, we didn't have rabbits running out in front. We took some of his load and slowed down. All he needed was for us to give him time to stay with us. At that point we changed our attitude and we became a team, not a bunch of individuals. At 13 years old, that was an influential part of my life . . .

Before starting a trek, Rangers hold a "shakedown" inspection with their crews. Nestled under a shade tree, one Ranger leads a crew through unpacking and repacking their backpacks. He makes sure they are taking only the essentials, shows them how to pack properly and how to keep weight to a minimum — ideally not more than 35 pounds per Scout — and how to distribute equally the common equipment furnished by Philmont: tent, fly, and cooking equipment.

"Who brought shampoo?" the Ranger asks his crew during their shakedown. "Hold it up, I want to see it!" Up shoot their arms. One boy holds a quart size container of shampoo. With a big grin the Ranger says, "I think you can save some weight by taking a little bottle of Camp Suds instead. It's biodegradable and highly concentrated. It will even wash your house, your friend's house, and everyone's house on your entire block for a year."

Fleabane on top of Phillips Mountain. This flowering plant was once believed to drive away fleas.

Before hitting the trail, Scouts make a commitment to conservation by signing and taking with them the Philmont Wilderness Pledge, which reads:

"Through good Scout camping, I pledge to preserve the beauty and splendor of the Philmont wilderness. I commit myself to:

1. A litter-free Philmont

2. An absence of graffiti

3. Conservation and proper use of water

4. Respect for trails and trail signs

5. Proper use of campsites."

THE PHILMONT WILDERNESS PLEDGE

Adult advisers willingly take a backseat at Philmont. They advise when needed, but they let their young Scouts lead the crew, make decisions on the trail, and set up and break camp.

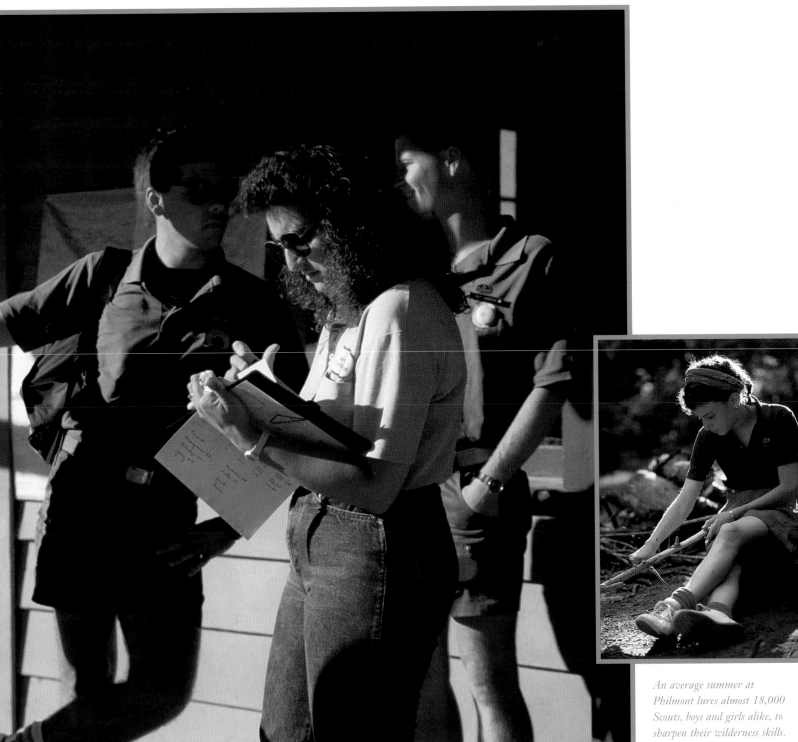

Before a trek, crew leaders and Rangers review important details. Once on the trail, decisions are largely left to each crew and crew leader; Rangers are there for assistance and teaching. The best Rangers lead from behind.

An average summer at Philmont lures almost 18,000 Scouts, boys and girls alike, to sharpen their wilderness skills. Hiking 50 or more miles in 12 days challenges the mind as much as the body.

And they practice what they pledge. You'll not see one scrap of paper on the ground anywhere at Philmont. On the trail, Scouts spend three hours doing a conservation project, a small way of repaying Philmont for the impact they have caused to the land.

When I got through the two weeks I knew I did something that most people in my school hadn't done—and at 13 I couldn't really explain it to them. It was a personal accomplishment. When I left after my first trip to Philmont all I thought about was wanting to get home, just to watch television. I didn't want to eat any more trail food, I was sick of getting up early. After about a month I started looking back, and I realized how much fun I had and how completely different it was for me than what I experience in Dallas. I viewed things differently from that point on. TV didn't hold the same appeal, it was so repetitious.

Years later when I joined the Philmont staff I saw a whole other dimension. Philmont completely changed my attitude about everything I do. Every time I helped a crew or a Scout, I learned vicariously by it. Philmont is what caused me to decide that the quality of what I was going to do for a living was more important than how much I got paid. Because of that, I chose education as a career. Looking back, that first trek as a 13-year-old was the best two weeks I have ever spent. It has been etched on my mind. That was thirteen years ago—half my life ago—and I remember it as vividly as anything that has happened since then.

PERCY PENTECOST, CHIEF RANGER

To Bates, Philmont is people. "We have people from all parts of the United States here, plus we'll have groups from five or six foreign countries. It's the most terrific melting pot you can imagine with kids from all over the world with different backgrounds. We had an entirely blind Scout crew one time. It's inspirational to see how everyone at Philmont—Scouts and staff alike—relate to one another. People here are able to get along and cooperate and work as a team, whereas back in their hometowns that might not be the case. Philmont weaves a magic spell on people, but part of the reason for that magic is the lure of the mountains. We are in the business of challenge. And it all ends up being an exhilarating experience for the Scouts. I think every crew that comes off the trail has the kind of feeling that says, 'We did it! It was tough, but we got through it and we're better for having had that type experience.'"

Backcountry camps are more than just a place to stop for the night on the trail. Each has a different theme with the staff trained to teach Scouts through demonstrations and actual hands-on experiences.

Today, some 150 Scouts from international locations experience Philmont; Dave Bates, director of program, hopes to see the number increase to 500.

This country is enchanted.

In all my life one of the things I'm most proud

of is the time I was a camp director at Philmont.

That's what this program is all about

—affecting the lives of kids.

STEPHEN ZIMMER,
DIRECTOR OF MUSEUMS AND CO-AUTHOR OF
PHILMONT, AN ILLUSTRATED HISTORY.

*Plenty of room, plenty of time. Youths explore not only the vastness
of the land, but the vastness of their own capabilities. From this vantage
point on upper Tooth Ridge at Cimarroncito, many Scouts see the world,
and themselves, as they never have before.*

*The changing face of Baldy, this time with
a shoulder blanket of snow in early spring.*

Chapter Three

North Country

Fewer than 100 years ago, miners toiled to find the "mother lode" on Baldy Mountain; today, Scouts toil to just reach the top of this 12,441-foot wind-swept, rocky-top giant. Where snarly miners once took $7 million in gold from Baldy and left their dilapidated buildings and abandoned equipment, today Scouts leave only their footprints, taking back golden memories of their trek to the top of the largest mountain on Philmont.

Philmont's jagged North Country is a rough blend of high mountains and high plateaus, laced with beautiful canyons steeped in history. In this region Scouts do everything from scale mountains to ride horses. At Indian Writings Camp, Scouts learn the prehistoric background of ancient Indians and participate in an archaeology project. At Dean Cow Camp, they become bona fide "rock jocks," learning to climb a steep wall and rappel down a real stomach-in-your-throat cliff. At French Henry they pan for gold, venture down an abandoned gold mine, and learn about blacksmithing. At Miranda they are taught how to pack a burro. At Ponil they ride horses, are taught to throw a rope, and learn about the West. At Pueblano the seasonal backcountry Philmont Scout staff takes on roles as loggers with the "Continental Tie and Lumber Company," showing campers log rolling, spartree "pole" climbing, and ax wielding. Scout crews compete in logging events, such as a log toss and crosscut sawing. And to top it off, Scouts have the opportunity to hike to the top of Baldy Mountain where the vistas and memories are as glittering as the minerals once sought after in this vast land.

Depending on their itinerary, Scouts can hike from 50 to 109 miles in a 12-day period that takes them through a few of the 27 backcountry camps, plus some 50 trail camps. The programs at the staffed camps vary but one thing is certain: they provide Scouts—boys and girls alike—with a fun, yet highly educational experience. Scouting leaders believe that experience is the best teacher; instead of lectures, Scouts see demonstrations; instead of boring presentations, Scouts get real-life, hands-on experiences.

This approach is by design, not by chance.

"The long-range dream for Philmont is to continue providing challenging, innovative, and exciting outdoor programs that help young people grow physically, mentally, and spiritually," says Dave Bates. "Young people today are more skilled, and we need to make sure our programs are challenging enough to meet their needs today as well as 10 years from now."

Philmont is special to me. When I was a camper here, it made me more self-confident, believe in myself, and believe in my friends. I wanted to return some of that to other campers and that's why I became a Ranger. I really love it here.

JENNY RIGDON,
20-YEAR-OLD PHILMONT RANGER FROM DAVENPORT, IOWA
WHO IS MAJORING IN MECHANICAL ENGINEERING AT THE
UNIVERSITY OF ILLINOIS.

C.M. "Chuck" Buenger, director and general manager of Philmont and director of high adventure programs for the Boy Scouts of America, says, "Most of what we do in Scouting is evolutionary rather than revolutionary. But we have changed our approach to the backcountry camps. We are conducting a bear research program, we are bringing in outside experts to talk with our staff about forestry, ecology, and archaeology, and we are starting a winter program for Scouts."

To Buenger, something inexplicable happens to Scouts in the backcountry. "When they return from a trek, they look back on it and say to themselves, 'I was up there and I did that!' Youth today have a lot of temptations and a lot of decisions to make. To me, opportunity knocks, but temptation leans on the doorbell. Young people who have confidence and good self-esteem are better prepared to make the right decisions about their lives. In a unique way, Philmont gives them that self-esteem. If we started out to design a piece of property to do these things, we would design a Philmont. It's providential that Waite Phillips bought this land and gave it to the Boy Scouts."

A hummingbird's wings move at 70 beats per second, enabling it to fly at speeds up to 180 mph.

When Philmont was called Philturn back in the 1940s, the original camp was at Ponil. Today Ponil is a western camp and is under the guidance of Mark "Freddie" Schweer, camp director and seasonal staff member.

Schweer, like most on the seasonal staff, came to Philmont as a Scout. And like many who become captivated by the Philmont spirit, he has joined the Philmont staff, returning each summer to work. To him, Philmont's physical challenge is so great that it becomes a mental challenge, and overcoming that mental barrier is hard. "Ranger or backcountry camp staff members see a lot of youth who really just need some extra encouragement, and that's what we try to do for them, just let them know that we believe in them."

The scenery is beautiful. Everybody thinks you go to Philmont to hike your soles off, but it's not the real reason—you come here for the different experiences, new adventures. Even the trail food is an adventure in itself. And how many places can you actually learn to pole like a logger, to pack a burro, and to carry everything on your back to support yourself—it's unbelievable. Here we are all a team, and if one person breaks down, we're all in a ditch, so we learn to cooperate and rely on others. People who go to Philmont seem to get a little more lease on life, more self-confidence, more abilities—and a great tan.

CLAYT O'NEILL,
16 YEARS OLD, TROOP 487, MEDIA, PENNSYLVANIA,
HEADING OUT OF PONIL CAMP.

Giving youth self-confidence is a big part of what Philmont is about. But that also extends to the adult advisers—Scoutmasters or assistant Scoutmasters—who bring their crews to these mountains. John Maxwell, Scoutmaster for Troop 969 in St. Charles, Missouri, and his assistant, Pat McDonald, were in the cantina at Ponil with their crew pouring down a pitcher of root beer. They looked hot and tired.

"We were sitting out in the middle of nowhere; literally, we were lost," Maxwell says. "We couldn't see a trail. So we sat down with our kids and looked at the map and pretty much determined where we were. There was no beefing or moaning. It was actually educational. We then made up our minds what we were going to do and we did it. But still, coming down that hill was kind of scary because when we got to the bottom I don't know how confident we really were that the trail was going to be there. But it was."

To Maxwell, what they did was a little like life. "Some people lie down when things get tough and others just get tougher as things get harder. They realize that life is going to be easy one day and tough the next, so we all have to choose what we're going to do about it."

That's part of what Philmont is about: teaching youth decision-making skills. And in doing so, Philmont causes people to open up, to evaluate, to change. "People grow up quickly here, and I'm talking about Scouts, advisers, and staff," says John Deal, director of Philmont's conservation program. Deal was a restaurant management major at the University of Florida. After spending two summers at Philmont he transferred to Texas A & M and became an environmentalist. He now has three degrees in the environmental science fields. "Philmont changed my perspective on the whole universe," he says. "This place affects your life."

To Deal, Philmont is about caring. "At Philmont, people open their hearts and their minds and try to do a really good job. Philmont brings out the best in people. The staff members here go out of their way to help kids see that what they're doing out here is going to last them a lifetime. A lot of the seasonal staff delay their careers just to come here every summer, and it's all for some kid who's a 5-foot 4-inch, 120-pound backpack with legs who's not sure why he's here in the first place. That's what we're about. This is the most real thing I'll probably ever do in my life."

At Miranda, a backcountry camp in Philmont's North Country, Scouts learn the detailed art of burro packing from seasonal staff members.

No, it's not a Scout in training for the telephone company—it's just part of the fun Scouts experience at Pueblano, a backcountry logging camp where they learn spartree "pole" climbing.

In some parts of Philmont, rain is an every-afternoon event during the summer. Scouts learn to live, hike, eat, sleep, and even have fun during these summer showers.

At Philmont you can pan for gold or scan for panorama at Wilson Mesa Lake.

This is God's country. One giant thunderhead over Wilson Mesa tells you why.

On top of old Baldy,
all covered with Scouts...

From this vantage point on top of Mount Phillips,
you can look north to Baldy Mountain. At 12,441
feet, Baldy is the highest point on Philmont and a
favorite hike for campers.

Virginia creeper

Tired dogs on top of Baldy.

There are more than 300 miles of trails at Philmont, about which one Scout said: "You need more rocks on your trails. There were points on the trail where it was actually dirt and the trails were level. This scared us to the point where we thought we were lost, but then we hit rocks and knew we were OK."

Woods

Did you ever walk into the woods alone?
Did you ever see the soft green moss
upon a rocky throne?
Did you ever watch the leaves
fall softly to the ground?
Did you ever listen to the murmur
of the little brook you found?
Did you ever hear the melodies
the wind makes when
it rustles in the trees?
Did you ever watch the snow birds
playing all around
Waiting for the snow to cover the ground?
If you saw and heard all this,
then you know
That the magic of the woods
Just grows and grows.

Esther Poppenhouse

*Scouts are taught what the Indians knew and practiced
—the balance between man, animals, and nature is
delicate and in constant danger of destruction.*

*Campfire songs and evening
entertainment tuck in the day
at backcountry camps.*

*Aspen Lake is a reflection, a mirror to the world.
Here clouds float by on blue-white wings taking
with them, if only for a moment, a Scout's dream
of what can be.*

Now I know the

secret of the making

of the best persons.

It is to grow in the

open air and to eat and

sleep with the earth.

▲▲

Walt Whitman

*North Ponil Canyon was once the home of Native Americans
known as the Anasazi from about 500 A.D. to 1000 A.D.*

Sunrise at Baldy Mountain beckons a climbing challenge to eager Scouts, but one who made the top said, "If God decided not to let me in heaven he'd make me climb Baldy one day and Shaffers the next for eternity."

The dawn is far away,

and the tired day

Rests on night's shoulders.

In the young twilight,

Sleep has wings tonight;

The campfire smolders.

▲▲

Samuel D. Bogan

Let the Coyotes Howl

At the end of each day, Scouts make camp and participate in the program at each backcountry location.

*"Two roads diverged in a wood, and I took the one less
traveled by and that has made all the difference..."
Surely Frost was speaking of Philmont when he penned
this years ago.*

The rufous-side towhee is a member
of the American finch family.

Melting snow gives Ponil Creek
a look that few see.

There is no such thing as a bad vista at Philmont.

"Thar's gold in them thar hills!"

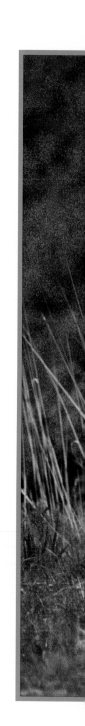

Scouts have much to look up to at Philmont.

Named for their mulelike ears,
mule deer are a common site at
Philmont.

It's said that the shooting star
grows where meteorites have landed.

Prehistoric petroglyphs dot the area in
north Ponil Canyon and are still a source
of mystery and intrigue today.

Scouting for Indian arrowheads.

At Indian Writings Camp, Scouts gather to hear how the first people in this area lived.

Next stop, Colorado! From this point above
Dan Beard Camp, Scouts can see clear into
Colorado and the foothills of the Rockies.

Viceroy butterfly

*Cold rain and hot cocoa...cold rain and
a good slicker...cold rain and a roaring fire.
Cold rain and indoors? Naah, too easy.*

*At Philmont, smiles
are passed on to others.*

*Ewells Park Camp, with Baldy
in the background.*

Artifacts come in different shapes and sizes like this miner's size 12's.

*Seasonal staff members make up the staff at Philmont's backcountry
camps. These young men and women not only dress the part, but act
the part, as in these prospectors at French Henry.*

Moss-covered rocks near Pueblano Camp.

Panning for gold at
French Henry.

Remnants of the mining days.

*Mining rails at French Henry that once carried
gold and other minerals from these mountains now
carry only memories on the wind.*

Sunrise at Webster Lake signals the start of another day for Philmont campers. With 12 days on the trail, they usually spend the late afternoon and night at a staffed backcountry camp. Each of the 27 backcountry camps has a different program, ranging from rock climbing to blacksmithing and from horse rides to fly fishing. Boredom is rare.

Chapter Four

Central Country

The yellow Chevy Suburban truck bounced over the rocks like a Slinky down a stairwell. Doug Palmer instinctively knows just when to turn the wheel to avoid the biggest rocks on the backcountry road to Cypher's Mine in the heart of Philmont's Central Country. Even still, everything not bolted to the inside of the truck—people included—is tossed around like dice in a gambler's cup.

As assistant program director for the Boy Scouts, Palmer makes frequent runs to the few backcountry camps that are accessible by road. Rounding an uphill turn, he spots a cinnamon bear in the meadow, not 50 yards away. It hasn't heard the truck and peacefully goes about its business, foraging for food.

Palmer stops and watches until the bear spots him and lumbers away into the trees.

Ute Gulch Commissary, a backcountry food pickup point and trading post for the Scouts, is one of Palmer's stops en route. Because most crews carry only a three- to four-day supply of food, Philmont has strategically placed backcountry commissaries where Scouts obtain a resupply of their basic foodpacks, and stock up on junk food at the trading post.

"Welcome to Phil-Mart and McPhil's," Rebekah Ellis chirps joyfully behind the counter of the wooden structure as she greets a group of thirsty Scouts. These kids have 'I-want-an-ice-cold-soda' blazoned across their lips. Their faces turn pale, their mouths drop open as Rebekah tells them there is no soda because there is no electricity. They unhappily settle for hot fruit drink and chalk up another lesson learned at Philmont—electricity isn't found everywhere in life, certainly not in the wilderness.

Philmont's young seasonal staff members at Ute Gulch and in other backcountry camps live a back-to-nature lifestyle. For three months they sleep in platform tents, do their own cooking on propane or wood burning stoves, get up at sunrise, go to bed when it's dark, and work nine days straight with three days off to return to Base Camp or hike around Philmont. And they love it.

Working in the backcountry is an escape from civilization. Back home, I have to wear a coat and a tie at work. There are no sounds of the city here. Things aren't as convenient; you learn to work for them at Philmont. It's really a neat sense of discovery.

TODD DEW,
SAWMILL CAMP DIRECTOR.

The hiking itineraries through Philmont's Central Country offer Scouts a smorgasbord of opportunities. At Cypher's Mine, they learn the craft of blacksmithing and walk back into an abandoned mine; at Cimarroncito they scale new heights by rock climbing; at Black Mountain the staff takes on the role of mountain men and teaches Scouts backwoods skills, black powder rifle shooting, and blacksmithing; at Clark's Fork they learn how to ride a horse and are treated to a rib-roaring chuck wagon dinner; at Harlan they learn how to stay atop a burro in a race that loses its seriousness before it ever begins; at Clear Creek, Philmont staffers portray real-life mountain men who have established the Rocky Mountain Fur Company. Here, wide-eyed Scouts learn how traps were used to catch beaver and muskrat and how these animals' hides were skinned and tanned.

"It's a lot of fun when the crews come in," says Todd Dew, camp director at Sawmill. "It's great when the crews are enthusiastic because we can really get into their mode. There are some days, though, when we don't feel like going to the rifle range, but all we have to do is just remember when we were campers and how excited we were—that gets us going."

Short tent, long Scout.

I've been to a lot of places, and I've found places where the scenery is prettier than here, but I've never been to a place that has the mixture of nature and people that Philmont has—the people here are incredible. Every night when we put on the Stomp at Cypher's Mine, I say to the Scouts: 'You probably think this is some of the hardest work you've ever done. Your body may be hurting some now, but I guarantee when you get back home, it may be a week, it may be a month, it may be next year, but you're going to look back on this as one of the best times of your lives.'

I did exactly that, and that's why I came back to be on staff at Philmont. I know most of the fellows who came out with my troop felt the same way, and that's what we're trying to instill in the youth who come to Philmont. I think we're successful because we have an incredible number who come back.

GREGG "BURRO" DAVIS,
CAMP DIRECTOR, CYPHER'S MINE.

Encounters with bears are a rarity at Philmont, but they do occur. Ryan Hanson, a Scout from Edmond, Oklahoma, says, "We were walking along the trail and a bear went by not 50 feet in front of me and it looked tan in color. Tim, who was behind me, said it was a sheep so I didn't think anything about it except I thought it was sure big for a sheep. Then it turned around and looked at us, and we go, 'A BEAR!' We all three went opposite directions." Rangers instruct Scouts what to do if they come upon a bear and how to use burlap "bear bags" at night to hoist food between two trees to keep it out of reach of bears and other hungry creatures.

It's not unusual for a Scout's parents to call Philmont and ask to speak to their son or daughter. Ali Oktay, director of Philmont's logistics department, says many often don't understand that Philmont is such an immense place. "We just can't step outside and say, 'Billy, it's for you.' But we try to be as accommodating as we can."

"Yesterday a woman called and said, 'My son's out there for a week. He told me to call.' She then started talking all at once. I asked her how old her son was and what he looked like. She said he was real big with dark hair and was 30 years old," Oktay says and laughs.

For real emergencies, Philmont's logistics department is better than an ICBM in locating its target. "We can find anyone within about 100 yards of where they are supposed to be," says Oktay, who is in his 10th season at Philmont. The massive trek board on the logistics office wall at Base Camp looks like something that General Eisenhower used to plan the landing at Normandy.

Philmont keeps a file on every Scout. "If anyone gets lost, we know what kind of wilderness experience they've had, their medical history, and their Scout rank—if they are an Eagle they should know what to do, and if they are a Tenderfoot they may not know what to do," Oktay says.

This information is of great help to PHILSAR, Philmont's Search and Rescue program which is called on to find a lost Scout, put out a fire, or help with other disasters, such as the downing of a private plane near Philmont in 1988. At a moment's notice, PHILSAR springs into action and can generally locate a Scout within a few hours.

To Oktay, Philmont is an elixir. "I first came to Philmont as a Scout in 1975. I was just lost in it at the time. Since then, I haven't stopped coming back. It's like home to me. It takes a different breed of person to leave the comforts of home, live in a tent for three months, and work with a lot of young people. The people here are some of the best you could have the opportunity to work with anywhere. A Philmont friend is a friend for life."

Rain at Wild Horse Camp.

Aspen trees are a vital source of food for many animals, especially the beaver. Bucks often scrape velvet from their antlers on the bark and bears use it to sharpen their claws. The quaking or trembling aspen is noted for its coin-size leaves that flutter in the wind.

*Sunrise from Comanche Peak echoes the words
of Tom Teece, Philmont staffer (1945-1948):
"The highest ambition in this life of mine is to
develop a soul like a stately pine..."*

Coming down the trail tell me what do I see?
Bear tracks, bear tracks looking back at me.
Better find a Ranger, boys, before it's too late
'Cause that bear's got all our food and he's headin' for the gate.

Well, he's big around the middle and he's broad across the rump
Running ninety miles an hour taking thirty feet a jump.
He ain't never been caught, he ain't never been treed.
Some folks say he's a lot like me.

CLASSIC SCOUTING SONG

The Tooth of Time Ridge is one of Philmont's most breathtaking features. Shaped by erosion, this double lacolith towers over Base Camp and is the Philmont symbol, not only on the Philmont patch, but in the minds of all who hike these magic mountains.

I was a Ranger in 1981
and had a day off so I went
on a hike. I was hiking ahead
of a crew so I got up in a tree
and was going to pretend
I was a bear. I had a cold
and after I growled at them
I coughed. The littlest kid in
the crew, he was really just
a pack with legs, turns around
to the others and yells,
'A bear! He's got a cold!'
I fell out of the tree laughing.

▲▲

John "Grizz" Deal.

At Cimarroncito, Scouts learn
to rappel down an "Oh, noooo!"
cliff, the kind that thrills Scouts
and would chill their mothers.

Scouts and patches go
together—this one of
Baden-Powell.

The view from Mount Phillips is worth the 11,711-foot climb. In the distance is the ever-present Baldy Mountain.

These two mountain women use the latest technology to dry clothes at Philmont.

*Igneous rocks resulting from volcanic activity cover
the landscape in lower Bonito Meadow. If these rocks
could speak, they'd have some tales to tell.*

Rise and shine! It's sunrise at Sawmill Camp.

Scouts learn to read the clouds at
Philmont by watching their ever-
changing moods.

Part of the Scouting experience is
learning about wildlife and reptiles.
Not all snakes at Philmont are as
harmless as this garter.

Scouts learn to not only shoot a .30-06 rifle, they learn to load the ammunition.

Mountain women relax after a long day's trek. Led by an experienced female Ranger, Philmont's Mountain Men/Women program involves six-day non-coed treks through the wilderness.

Scouts don't always strike it rich (actually, none has so far), but they don't leave empty-handed either. This Scout and his adviser examine a piece of ore from a mine.

At Dean Cow Camp, Scouts become bona fide "rock jocks" as they learn the fine art of mountaineering, teamwork, and overcoming obstacles, both internal and external.

Wanderlust brings Scouts to Sawmill Canyon,
and wonderment keeps them there.

Nature has its own art, as in this
close-up of an aspen tree.

These Scouts are having the times of their lives.
They're just too tired to realize it now.

*Now he knows the reason behind the Scout motto,
'Be prepared.' This sudden hailstorm on the hike to
Mount Phillips causes one adviser to take shelter
as best as he can.*

John Muir could have been speaking about the Tooth of Time when he wrote:
"Climb the mountains and get their good tidings. Nature's peace will flow into you
like sunshine flows into the trees. The winds will blow their own freshness into
you and the storms their energy while cares will drop off like autumn leaves."

Winter at Cathedral Rock shows a side of Philmont that Scouts don't see. A new winter program is being added to enable small groups to experience winter camping and survival techniques.

The rugged grandeur around Cimarroncito.

Beauty in Winter
Did you ever walk into the woods
When everything was brown and
bare.
Did you say how ugly everything
was this time of year.
You must be mistaken, there's
so much beauty there.
Did you ever look at the
great structure of a tree
That's beauty, at least it is to me.
Did you look at the formation
of so many rocks
the soft green moss that clings to
them
like the fur upon a fox.
Did you ever hear the rustle
of the brown dry leaves
When out of the cold fresh air
comes a little breeze.
There's beauty everywhere
If you'll just take a look
For God made this world
Just like a fairy book.

Esther Poppenhouse

Backcountry staff members dress their parts so well over the course of the summer they almost become their roles.

At Clear Creek, a Philmont program coordinator shows Scouts how to load and shoot a black-powder rifle.

A lone pine branches out
into aspen territory.

*Backcountry staff members
at Cypher's Mine dress, talk,
act, and become the roles of
miners of yesterday as they
teach Scouts about early-day
mining life at Philmont.*

Webster Lake

Give a Scout a hammer and stand back! Here, Scouts try their hand at blacksmithing.

Evening, lantern light, a cup of coffee, and good friends...ahh. At night, backcountry staff members share stories of today and map out agendas for tomorrow.

Ready…aim…
(We're black powder
shooting at Black
Mountain Camp)
…fire!

Scouts learn to balance
their day—in more ways
than one.

Scouts learn to load a black
powder rifle at Crater Lake.

A backcountry staff member teaches
Scouts about early-day trapping methods
at Clear Creek Camp.

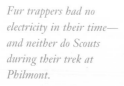

Fur trappers had no
electricity in their time—
and neither do Scouts
during their trek at
Philmont.

*Restored to authenticity, this cabin at the Rocky Mountain
Fur Company at Clear Creek Camp transports Scouts to the
mountain man era.*

Scouts descending Mount Phillips.

Whew! We made it!
On top of Mount Phillips—
11,711 feet.

"Mom!

Philmont's not

just some shack

in the woods."

▲▲

Scout

overheard

on the

pay phone.

*The Greek philosopher Heraclitis said you cannot
step in the same river twice because the river and
you are both constantly changing. At Philmont, Rayado
Creek represents the change that many Scouts make
after their Philmont experience.*

Chapter Five

South Country

The names of camps in Philmont's South Country slip off your tongue like a Scout's boot off a rock on the trail: Urraca, Abreu, Beaubien, Fish Camp, Lover's Leap, Apache Springs.

From the lush, high mountain meadow of Beaubien to the churning waters of Fish Camp, from the time-forgotten Rayado Canyon to the serene Abreu, South Country is a blend of the rough and the gentle, the intriguing and the reposed.

It's late afternoon at Beaubien and the sky is as gray and crumbly as a Scout's three-day-old wool hiking socks. At 9,300 feet, Beaubien is a western lore camp, tucked in the mountains amidst a meadow sprinkled with white and yellow wildflowers. Here, horses graze contentedly and Scouts roam freely.

This is the kind of country where you'd expect to see Hoss and Little Joe ride out to meet you as you come in off the trail. Instead, 6-foot 4-inch Willie Hittson, Beaubien's camp director, strides out of the cabin, bolts down the steps and greets a group of Scouts with an enthusiastic, "Welcome to Beaubien!"

After asking about their trek, his eagle-eyes spot a watch on the wrist of a young camper. "That's a great watch you have. By the way, did you know that brightly colored watches like that attract bears at night?" he asks in a serious tone. The two enter into a good-natured back and forth 'you're-kidding-no-I'm-not', but the look on the Scout's face makes you think that tonight he'll do his good deed for the day and put the watch in his pack. Just to be safe.

"When you first greet Scouts the main job is to get them excited about what is going on," says Hittson, who first came to Philmont as a young Scout in the early 1970s. "It's critical to have a good time with the kids and to joke around with them. At Beaubien we're a western camp. We're supposed to be like real cowboys,

just like the staff at French Henry is supposed to be like real miners. If we do a good job of our interpretation, it will impress them. I once had a Scout wait to get me alone to ask me if I was a real cowboy. 'Well, as a matter of fact,' I said, 'I'm not. I'm a college student, but we do have some wranglers who are real cowboys.'"

To Hittson, there are two qualities that he wants Scouts to leave with as a result of their Philmont experience: first, a oneness with nature to inspire care for the land no matter where they go, and second, fun while they're here. "Every now and then, one of the interpretive programs might spark their interest. I've heard of kids getting interested in something like black-smithing, horseback riding, or rock climbing after learning about it here."

When Scouts finish their treks, they go back home changed. At Philmont they had to learn to cooperate with 8 to 10 other people for 12 days. They carried their own weight. They cooked their own meals. They survived lightning storms, rainstorms, and steep trails. This is still a wilderness. Kids can get lost and the weather can change suddenly so they have to learn to work together and cooperate.

BARRY OXLEY,
PROGRAM COUNSELOR AT BEAUBIEN.

Scouts who have Beaubien on their back-country itinerary in South Country are taught to ride a horse, throw a rope, and brand. (Instead of branding a cow, they singe either the Philmont cattle brand or Scout Ranch brand on their boot or hat.) At night, they are treated to a chuck wagon cookout and an evening of songs and jokes under a star-filled sky.

The nine-member Beaubien staff and wranglers are a unique lot who live a real Ponderosa lifestyle. They have three cabins—one where they eat their meals, another where those with the interpretative program sleep, and a bunkhouse by the corral where the wranglers sleep. For three months they live without electricity, using propane for cooking and kerosene to light their cabins at night.

On any evening, you can find advisers on the porch of the cabin drinking cups of cowboy coffee, telling of their day's experiences; directly in front, Scouts challenge one another to a game of horseshoes.

Lunchtime! This longtail weasel has his eyes peeled.

"One of my Scouts already has an application form filled in to come back to Philmont as a staff member," says one adviser from Kentucky. "You never know what will happen to Scouts as a result of going through Philmont. Some of them say it's too tough, but once they get through it, they begin to think differently. When they get home they say, 'It was a piece of cake. I *walked* up that mountain—some of the guys were dragging, but not me!' The truth is, most of us advisers are the ones dragging!"

Inside the cabin, Ernie Thomas, the cook for the camp staff, is making corn bread and stew and something out of leftovers that defies description but tastes great. On the wall is this sign: "Only a darned fool would argue with a skunk, a woman, or the Beaubien cook." But one look at Ernie's constantly smiling face tells you that you'd be hard pressed to get an argument from him. Later, around the table, the staff sits down to the evening meal, always started with the Philmont Grace. These young men have been together just three weeks and already act as if they have been long friends. They become the roles they play so well that it's easy to forget they are not full-time cowboys and wranglers: Willie, at 28, the self-proclaimed "old man" in the group, wants to be a doctor; Barry Oxley, who wears an Australian bush hat and plays the harmonica, is studying for an MBA; Jim Glover, who puts coffee in just about everything, is a student at Texas A&M; Mark Kerr, who is personable, quick-witted, and reads books every night by flashlight on his cot, is studying to be an architect; Dave Angel, who has a slow drawl as entertaining as his stories; John Alexander, who is quiet, yet injects the right point at the right time; and Blain Hintze, the youngest, who is the spitting image of Tom Cruise.

Philmont is like a second home to many, especially those who come back on staff. You're family here, and we all strive to get back every summer somehow, some way.

ERNIE THOMAS,
COOK AT BEAUBIEN.

When Scout crews leave Beaubien's enchanted meadow, they often hike to Fish Camp, the site of Waite Phillips's original fishing cabin where he entertained friends and guests. Today, Scouts tour the historic site and learn how to tie their own trout flies—then put those to test in the waters of the Agua Fria Creek.

Other camps in South Country offer Scouts a wide variety of activities: At Abreu, they mix clay, straw, and sand and turn it into an adobe brick. After it has dried, they place it on a wall of a casa being built entirely by Scouts. At Crater Lake, they become part of the Continental Tie and Lumber Company where they take on the role of a logger for a day. At Miner's Park, they scale heights, learning how to safely climb and rappel. At Urraca, they go through a series of outdoor teamwork exercises, each designed to test their ability to cooperate and overcome obstacles, both real and imaginary, such as how to get 10 Scouts over a 12-foot wall and do it without talking or gesturing. At Apache Springs, they see how the Jicarilla Apache Indians lived, and have the opportunity to make arrowheads, grind corn, and even enjoy a Jicarilla sauna.

No matter which camp is on their itinerary through South Country, each location strives to give Scouts a growth experience. Scouts grow physically by learning how to hike faster and further and complain less while carrying a heavy pack from one backcountry camp to another. But what is truly amazing is the mental growth. Leadership comes from within each crew. Advisers are asked to play a secondary role—they are there for emergencies, not to provide leader-ship. The leadership bubbles up out of each Scout crew of 13- to 16-year-olds.

On the trail, Scouts and their advisers find that their biggest decisions center around where to put their next footstep, how to get dinner cooked, and making sure they're not going to die of hypothermia. To John Deal, director of conservation, Philmont gives them a chance to "get out of video drive, so they'll know there's something going on besides what's being flashed across MTV. We give them time away from what they're used to. Maybe that's the most important thing they get at Philmont—time."

For some kids, a trail ride at Beaubien represents two first-time events—their first time on a horse and their first time to wake up this early.

Mark Kerr, a seasonal staff member at Beaubien, prepares branding irons that Scouts use to emblazon the Philmont brand on their boots—and other clothing.

Tools of the trade.

When you're hot, you're hot. These young Scouts learn about branding from a backcountry staff member.

Like mailmen, Cavalcade cowboys bring in the pack horses rain or shine at Beaubien.

*The sunrises at Beaubien are
rivaled only by the sunsets.*

*An early morning trail ride
at Beaubien lets Scouts see
a part of Philmont from a
different angle.*

Headin' home! Philmont Cavalcade riders sport a flag as they return home.

Wrangler locker room.

*A Philmont wrangler keeps a
paternal eye on Scouts during a ride.*

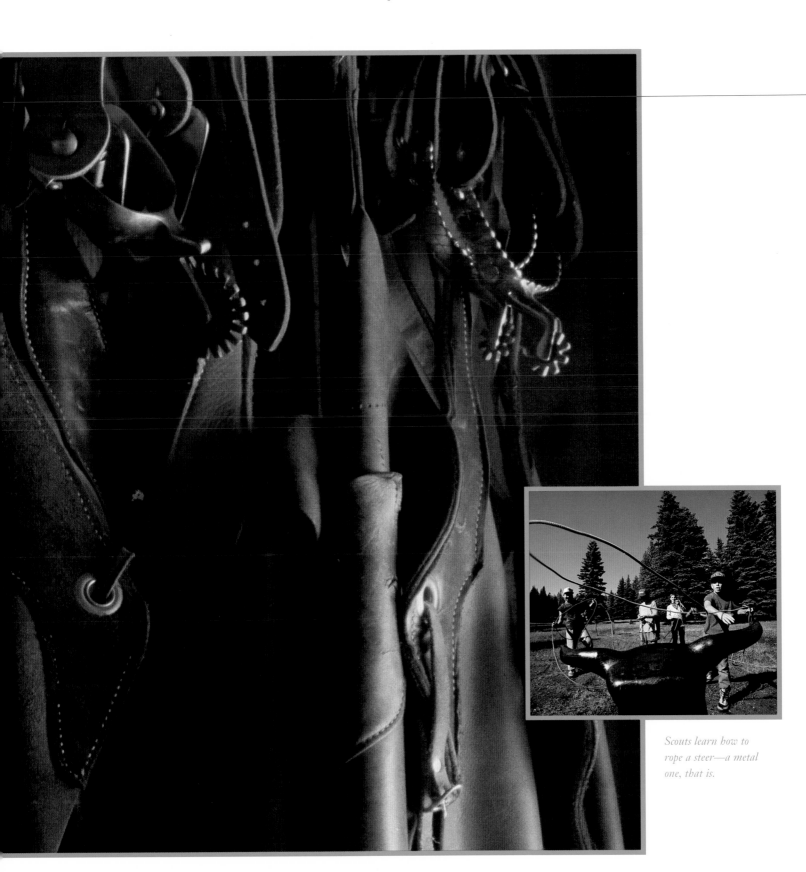

Scouts learn how to rope a steer—a metal one, that is.

Willie Hittson, camp director at Beaubien, entertains Scouts each evening with his fiddle playing.

At the close of the campfire at Beaubien, Camp Director Willie Hittson tells Scouts this story:

A rancher near Rayado Town died, and they had an auction to sell his belongings. Everybody in town came out for the event. The auctioneer came across an old, dusty, worn-out looking fiddle.

"Who will give me a dollar for this fine fiddle?" he asked as he started the bid. The crowd didn't seem too interested in it.

He finally got a dollar bid, and he was working the crowd real hard, but could get no more than two dollars. Just as he was about to close the bidding a fellow came down, picked up the fiddle, blew off the dust, put it under his chin, tuned it a little and started to play. Out came the sweetest, most beautiful music. He finished the tune, put the fiddle down, and went back to his seat.

The auctioneer didn't know what to think of this, but started the bidding again. "Who'll give me five dollars for this fine fiddle?" He immediately got it. Pretty soon he had a 10 dollar bid and then a 30 dollar bid. Before he knew it, it was up to 100 dollars!

The bidding skyrocketed because someone came down, tuned and played the fiddle. But it was the same fiddle as the one that could only muster a two dollar bid. The fiddle didn't look like much and people didn't pay much attention to it until someone came along and did something with it.

Your experience at Philmont is like that, too. You have these mountains and difficult hiking trails, and it rains and at times you may have aches and pains. But remember: What you get out of your time at Philmont depends on what you put into it. Just like the fiddle, there is a tune inside each of you just waiting to be played.

▲▲

Standing tall is what Philmont is all about.

Lower Bonita Meadow

A big buck just after removing velvet from his horns.

A young doe ever alert in the tall grass.

Wherever you go, there you are. Now just where are we?

Philmont is a place where success is emphasized.

Two days ago a 14-year-old from Colorado

got homesick and wanted to go home.

Todd Conklin, coordinator of camping services,

went up to talk with him.

"I told him he couldn't go home,"

Conklin says, matter-of-factly.

The boy started crying and his eyes got real

big and he said, "Really?"

"Yeah, you can't go home," Conklin responded.

"I don't think you need to go home. I think that

you can work through this problem. You've got

to work through it sometime, and Philmont is

a pretty good place to do it. But I'll tell you what,

I'll make a deal with you: If you stay out tomorrow

I'll have the chaplain meet you at the next camp

and if you still want to leave, then you can."

The next day the chaplain came back without

the boy. He said he was having tons of fun.

*At Philmont, ground
squirrels are called
"minibears."*

Water speeds down Rayado Canyon like a race car at Watkins Glen—and next to it Scouts hike from one back-country camp to another in Philmont's South Country.

At Abreu, Scouts learn to construct an adobe casa. Mixing a batch of adobe mud, they pack it into forms to mold bricks. When the bricks dry, they will be used to construct a house and adobe oven.

Inspiration Point

You could bring in a group
of 40 kids whose gear was stolen
in their U-haul on the way here
and they'd still be out on the trail
the next day fully equipped.
"There's nothing we can't do at
Philmont if we have three
hours notice!"

▲▲

Todd Conklin,
coordinator of camping services.

That's another fine fix! Part of the
Philmont experience is learning
to make the right decisions: where to
put the next foot, for starters.

Turkeys are wild at Philmont.
They were once proposed by
Benjamin Franklin to be the
national bird.

Picturesque scapes for great escapes. Here—Rayado Creek.

I want to go back to Philmont

Where the old Rayado flows,

Where the rain comes a seepin'

In the tent where you're a-sleepin'

And the waters say hello.

I want to wake up in the morning

With my socks all wringing wet,

For it brings back fond memories,

That a Ranger can't forget.

I want to hike once more the canyon floor

From Scribblins to Old Camp,

With my pack sack a-creakin',

With my back with sweat a-reekin',

And my legs beginning to cramp.

I want to hike again with such great men

As made those famous treks,

From Beaubien to Porky

And from Cito to Car-Max.

▲▲

Ranger Song

Inspiration Point. The perfect cure for claustrophobia.

Scouts may get butterflies
on the obstacle course, but they
gain a big helping of confidence
after it's over.

Tiger swallowtail butterfly

A Scout is never lost, as long as he has a compass.
A map and companions don't hurt either.

Wildflowers in the wilderness.
This dwarfed crimson columbine
is from the buttercup family.

Proof positive: This Ranger eats trail food
and he's still smiling!

These young elk are sparring to establish dominance.

The winter wonderland
of Urraca Creek.

Rayado Creek in spring.

Rayado Creek in fall.

Garcia Mesa

On the trail to Fish Camp.

A staff member at Black Mountain had a beautiful pocket watch, but he didn't have a chain for it. He kept it in the front bib of his overalls. One day he was in the latrine, and the watch fell out of his overalls down through a crack in the floor and got caught on a little root. He was quite upset over this, so I encouraged him to get it out. He borrowed a little pocket fisherman from this fellow and there he was, in the latrine, fishing to get his watch back. A Scout came by and saw him fishing down the hole and said, 'Are you catching anything?'

▲▲

By the way, he did get his watch back.

Waite Phillips built Fish Camp Lodge as a place to entertain visiting dignitaries, providing them with complete fishing equipment and outfits. Today, Scouts tour the rustic lodge.

There is a fine art to tying a fly.

*It's one thing to tie a fly
during daylight; the real test
comes by lantern.*

*Scouts must have
learned how to stretch
from the aspen tree.*

The Kit Carson Museum
is just seven miles south of
Philmont and a popular
attraction for visitors.

Lover's Leap..."Climb the mountains and get their good tidings. The wind will blow their own freshness into you, and the storms, their energy, while cares will drop away from you like the leaves of autumn."—John Muir

At Abreu, Scouts see demonstrations on weaving.

Jack n' Jill went up the hill... Scouts learn cooperation and find ways to make a hard job easier.

*At Abreu, Scouts try their skill—
or lack of it—at burro racing.*

*Nothing beats a hard day
on the trail like a root beer
at the Abreu cantina.*

At Apache Springs Camp, Scouts learn how the
Jicarilla Apache lived on the land that is now Philmont.

Rocky Mountain iris presents a floral pageantry at Philmont.

The Indians had their own version of the sauna—it's called the sweat lodge, and these Scouts find out just how hot it can be.

Scouts try their luck at making arrowheads.

For food,

For raiment,

For life,

For opportunity,

For friendship and fellowship,

We thank Thee, O Lord.

Amen

▲▲

Philmont Grace

*Church service is offered each Sunday at Philmont.
Philmont has chaplains from six religions who travel
the backcountry offering assistance.*

Cathedral Rock:
A spire of splendor
in the sky.

"All paths lead nowhere, so it is
important to choose a path that has heart."
—*Carlos Castaneda*

Chapter Six

Super Activities

Rayado

A Rayado Trek is like a marathon in the mountains, only in hiking boots with a 35-pound backpack. In case you didn't read the small print, it lasts 15 days and covers anywhere between 100 to 200 miles, depending on the chutzpah of the crew.

Scouts who are attracted to the Rayado adventure believe in no pain, no gain, and go in search of the utmost physical challenge. This is not your standard Philmont outing. Scouts discover that it's as much a mental journey as it is a physical journey.

A Rayado crew consists of 10 to 12 Scouts who come to Philmont not as a ready-made crew from the same Scout troop, but as individuals from all parts of the country. In the beginning, they do not know each other; when they leave Philmont, they will have formed lifelong friendships. They are led by two elite Rangers with no adult supervision. They are told little about the program, except it will be challenging and it would be wise to get more exercise than a walk around the block before arriving at Philmont.

"The Rayado program is probably the best program at Philmont," says George Bach, a training Ranger who will be a sophomore at Center College outside Louisville, Kentucky. "The challenge is the unknown part of it. While we never divulge what takes place, I can say that we put Scouts in situations that build their self-confidence and leadership."

Paul Kapfer, seasonal staff member from Griswold, Iowa, is responsible for the Rayado program. To him, Scouts leave the Rayado challenge with "a sense for what they can do and for who they are."

Earlier this year Chuck Buenger, director and general manager of Philmont, told Kapfer and the other Rayado Rangers that "the most important part of the Rayado program should be to help young men and women develop a strong sense of self-esteem, so they know what their own values are and what their criteria for making decisions are."

To Kapfer, this means helping them with the "ability to stand and decide matters in life for themselves rather than letting other things be imposed on them."

Kapfer and his Rayado Rangers accomplish this through a number of strategies. First is the very nature of the Rayado program. Instead of knowing their itinerary in advance, Rayado Scouts discover the program in the wilderness. Instead of always sticking to the trails, Rayado Scouts do off-trail hiking, learning heavy-duty orienteering skills. They often camp in undesignated areas, practicing no-trace, low-impact camping methods. For confidence building, the rock climbing staffs at Cimarroncito, Miner's Park, and Dean Cow set up special challenging climbs on mind-boggling pitches. Afterward, their self-esteem is as high as the peaks they scale.

A Ranger was sleeping under the stars one night on a Rayado Trek. He woke before day-break to discover that a rattlesnake had made its bed on top of his sleeping bag, the warmest place around. Neither the snake nor the Ranger moved for at least two hours until the sun came up and the trek coordinator came over and scared the rattler away. The Ranger said he had never been so scared and so motionless in his life.

Beyond blister-breaking hikes, the Rayado program teaches Scouts leadership and decision-making skills. "I'm encouraging Rayado Rangers to have the group select a different leader each day so every Scout has the experience of leading a crew," Kapfer says. "To me, leadership is the most important skill in the outdoors. You can know knot-tying skills inside and out, but it's decision-making that is critical—knowing when to go ahead and climb and when it's not a good idea." As part of this, at the end of each day Rayado crews discuss the decisions they felt were most important on the trek and talk about why they were made and how those decisions could have been made differently.

On Rayado Treks, young men and young women (no coed treks) learn to work together to cope with unexpected challenges, be receptive to ideas other than their own, and find opportunity out of diversity. The objective is for these newly acquired experiences and skills to carry over into a Scout's life away from Philmont.

The Rayado program is more than just hiking the Vibram soles off your boots. It's a journey beyond physical barriers. It's a journey into self-analysis, reflection, and introspection, where youth are able to see themselves as they are and as the best they can and want to be.

"Our goal," Kapfer says, "is to make each participant's experience the most fun and exciting time in his or her life."

The bull snake is one of the largest snakes in the U.S., often reaching a length of nine feet.

"You look like you could use a break!" That's a line adult advisers use on Scouts when they want to stop for a rest. Scouts carry 35-pound backpacks for 12 days, sharing the weight of group equipment and supplies.

It's not Iwo Jima, but these Scouts celebrate their 12,441-foot hike up old Baldy.

Mountain Men and Women

In addition to regular twelve-day expeditions, Philmont offers special six-day hiking treks, called Mountain Men and Mountain Women.

These expeditions are for 13- to 20-year-old men and women organized into male or female crews of five to eight. Each trek is led by a Philmont Ranger.

Trail Crews

To help preserve the wilderness, Philmont has developed a Trail Crew program where older Scouts and Explorers spend sixteen days doing a backcountry work project.

John Deal, seasonal staff member who is director of conservation, says, "They work on programs ranging from clearing trails, erosion control, and reconstruction—it's an ecologist's dream."

After they complete their project, Trail Crew members are rewarded with a free High Adventure Expedition.

Garcia Meadows abloom with blossoms of snow.

*Wild roses waft their
fragrance in the wind.*

Cavalcades

For those who would rather ride than walk, the Philmont Cavalcades program provides just the ticket. Cavalcades offer youth the chance to experience the peaks and valleys of Philmont from the back of a horse instead of from the soles of their boots.

While the initial advantage is not having to pack a 35-pound backpack, the Scouts in the Cavalcades program are drawn to it for a deeper reason: they get to ride and care for a horse for an eight-day backcountry expedition in the same tradition as the famous fur trappers who first explored these mountains.

Scouts in the Cavalcades program learn how to ride a horse like the mountain men of old, navigate by horseback, care for and feed their horses, and work together as a team to accomplish goals.

And spending eight days in the saddle gives them blisters where they've never had them before!

Two good friends at Beaubien prepare for a morning ride.

Mountain Women signing in at Clear Creek.

Trail food sounds good—

beef stroganoff or an enchilada dinner—

but it all basically tastes the same.

Kids boil a pot of water and then

dump everything in it because

it's more efficient for everyone to

cook in one pot.

Unfortunately, everything has

the same thick texture.

It's noisy food.

They plop it on their plates

and they look at it.

I really think there's a moment

when everyone looks at their

plates and wonders if they're

supposed to eat it or if they already have.

▲▲

Todd Conklin,

coordinator of camping services.

End of the ride—wet, tired, hungry—and a little sore.

"He was part of my dream, of course—
but then I was part of his dream, too."
—Lewis Carroll, Through the Looking-Glass

Wilson Mesa

Scouts on a trek from Black Mountain.

Philmont has a unique Trail Crew

program where youth come to spend

two weeks doing conservation work

throughout the summer.

John Deal, director of conservation,

says, "They work on programs ranging

from clearing trails, erosion control,

revegetation, and reconstruction—

it's an ecologist's dream.

Afterward we give them a free

10-day trek."

▲▲

*Everything worth preserving takes time and
energy, as these Trail Crew members experience.*

I'm tired. My feet hurt. Who put all these rocks here?
Are we there yet? The hike to the top of Baldy brings out
the best, and then some, in everyone.

*Parry primrose flowers on top of
Baldy show that life is everywhere,
you just have to look for it.*

*Philmont from an eagle's eye. To the left is
Base Camp, to the right is Villa Philmonte
and the Philmont Training Center complex.
Tooth Ridge is in the background.*

Chapter Seven

Philmont Training Center

When business leaders want to learn the latest business strategies they go to training programs at the nation's premier business schools. When volunteer Scout leaders want to learn the latest Scouting strategies they come to one place: the Philmont Training Center, the top-notch training school of Scouting.

Located just across the road from the Philmont Scout Ranch and on the same grounds as Villa Philmonte, the Philmont Training Center is an educational mecca for volunteer Scout leaders from across the nation. They come—5,000 over the course of the summer season—to attend conferences and participate in a phantasmagoria of courses and workshops on topics ranging from developing a quality troop to Scouting for the handicapped, and from strengthening Boy Scouting to Cub Scout den leaders' workshops.

Attendance is by invitation only. "The selection of participants is up to the 410 local Boy Scout councils," says Forrest McVicar, director of the Training Center. "At the Training Center, these volunteer leaders learn that they really are a part of a major national organization. By participating with other volunteer leaders from across the country, they are able to exchange ideas and information. They leave this place inspired, just like the kids do over at the Philmont Scout Ranch."

Volunteers who come to the Training Center are encouraged to bring their families and make a vacation out of the trip. "We have a family program for everyone from nursery age children to spouses," says McVicar, a 30-year veteran of the Boy Scouts of America organization. "While the volunteer Scout leader attends training programs, his or her spouse can attend handicrafts workshops, take nature hikes, and tour the surrounding area. There are numerous programs for children, and if they are the ages of

Cub Scouts or Boy Scouts, they can participate in the Rocky Mountain Scout Camp. This camp is a complete and separate operation from Philmont, devoted to youth whose parents are in the Training Center. Kids stay at the Rocky Mountain Scout Camp the entire week. They can also participate in the Mountain Men/Mountain Women six-day backpacking expedition. It's just a super experience for the entire family."

In 1989 there were 44 week-long training conferences, including an all-important Advancement Conference, led by volunteer Scout leader George Boyett, from College Station, Texas. "This is the Big Bang of Scouting," he says. "We've taken a long look at Scouting, and we're making some milestone changes...." The three major aspects of those changes involve making Scouting a more outdoor experience, providing an outdoor adventure program, and a Varsity athletic program for older Scouts.

"Studies have shown that youth need more challenging programs," says Boyett, who is on Scouting's National Task Force Committee. "They can only tie so many knots. We lose kids by not getting them out-of-doors fast enough. We're trying to instill that very message in the volunteer leaders who come to the Training Center."

Charles "Chuck" Walneck, chairman of the National Training Task Force from Cary, Illinois, says that when he first came to the Training Center in 1981 he came back inspired and refreshed. "There shouldn't be a more difficult way of doing things, there should be an easier way, and the Training Center teaches us the easier way."

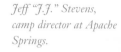

Jeff "J.J." Stevens, camp director at Apache Springs.

Boyett is enthused by the variety of programs offered at the Training Center. "Just this week we have an absolutely dynamite program called Outdoor Living Skills. The group has no classroom. Every morning they leave with a pack and their food and they teach as they go. If it rains, all the better; in fact, they even do a little rain dance so they can demonstrate how to teach Scouts to do things in the rain."

Walneck is enthusiastic about the National Junior Leader Instruction Camp where he says, "the rubber meets the road. We could teach adults everything about running a program, but if the program is structured properly the baton will be passed to the youth. The NJLIC is something special because that's where we teach youth to become junior leaders."

To Boyett, the objective of the Training Center is to provide first-class training to volunteer Scout leaders so they can keep the Scouting tradition alive and progressing with the times. "We want to get more kids in Scouting so they can learn and have fun in the outdoors. By doing so, they will see how the Scout Law applies to everyday decisions they make and will make in the future. That's we offer—for youth to be able to make the right decisions about their lives. The programs of the 1970s don't work for us now. That's why we're making some progressive changes that are exciting, in the best interests of the kids and that keep Scouting's traditions alive. After all, our basic mission is the same today as it was 75 years ago—we're still trying to build character, citizenship, and make youth mentally, morally, and physically fit."

Baldy Mountain skyscrapers.

*Adult advisers become
kids again.*

*Part of what makes Philmont special are the
challenges Scouts overcome during their 12-day
adventure. At Urraca, they must negotiate an
obstacle course, often without speaking, that requires
them to work as a team and not as individuals.*

Dr. David Nilsson has been
bringing Scouts to Philmont
for 35 years.

Between a rock and a hard place.
Rock climbing at Cimarroncito teaches
youth to get a grip in a tight spot.

On top of Urraca Mesa.

A Philmont Ranger with full gear.

Philmont Trivia

Philmont is the largest organized camping area in the world.

It's believed only the U.S. Army uses more trail food than Philmont.

There are 315 miles of trails, 27 backcountry staff camps with programs, and more than 50 unstaffed trail camps.

Four million Scouts and Scout leaders are registered in the United States.

The first Scouts went through Philmont in the summer of 1939.

526,000 Scouts have gone through Philmont in 50 years.

A record 19,293 Scouts went through Philmont in 1968.

Some 14,572 Scouts went through Philmont in 1989.

The average Scout carries a 35-pound pack and hikes 75 miles in 12 days.

14,572 Scouts at Philmont hiked a total of 1,050,000 miles in 1989, carrying a total of 42,000 pounds of gear on their backs. This is equal to 42 trips around the world.

Total number of miles hiked by all Scouts who have gone through Philmont in its 50-year history: 38,400,000. This is equal to 160 trips to the moon.

In 1989, Scouts contributed 42,000 hours to conservation projects.

Philmont comprises 214 square miles or 137, 493 acres.

The value of Philmont is $54 million.

The shortest itinerary trek is 50 miles.

Hummingbird moth visits a thistle.

Pausing to celebrate: On the rim of Rayado Canyon.

At Philmont, ground squirrels are called "minibears" and fruit drink is called "bug juice."

More than 700,000 meals are served in three months of operation.

The average Scout loses between one to three gallons of fluid a day hiking the trails at Philmont.

In 1988, Scouts consumed:
190,500 cups of cocoa
119,300 beef jerky strips
93,000 beef sticks
84,000 cans of peaches
80,000 boxes of crackers
43,072 cans of 'spreadables'
 (chicken, tuna)
42,192 tubes of squeeze cheese
112,848 cans of pop
800 pounds of popcorn
80,000 ice cream cones

From April 1 to May 15, nine people in the Philmont Commissary pack 153,000 food items in plastic bags.

Scouts mailed 81,589 postcards in 1988 and bought 14,385 T-shirts.

Philmont employs over 600 seasonal staff members each summer.

Philmont's permanent full-time staff consists of 50 people, including those who operate the Training Center.

Philmont gives up to $150,000 in scholarships to almost 500 Scouts through the Waite Phillips Scholarship Fund.

The Philmont Scout Ranch has the following livestock: 220 cows, 200 calves, 80 heifers, 15 bulls, 200 horses, 135 buffalo, and three full-time cowboys.

Philmont has 1,972 tents, 684 backpacks, and 1,035 bear bags.

The elevation at Philmont ranges from 6,500 feet to 12,441 feet.

On any given day at Base Camp during the summer season, there are 600 Scouts —
300 arriving; 300 leaving.

Photo Credits

ALLTON	100, 101, 144, 145, 175
COX	18, 19, 43, 46, 47, 56, 57, 59, 84, 85, 86, 91, 97, 126, 128, 129, 130, 171
GROTH	61, 68, 69, 70, 71
HALPERN	14, 15, 38, 57, 58, 62, 64, 67, 81, 90, 94, 95, 98, 99, 106, 124, 125, 131, 174
MAURER	67, 89, 93, 102, 103, 104, 105, 112, 120, 121, 156, 157
MEANS	44, 52, 54, 56, 57, 59, 61, 63, 65, 72, 73, 74, 75, 147, 153, 162
OVERTURF	34, 35, 54, 55, 76, 98, 138, 158, 159
POPPENHOUSE	Cover, 6, 10, 11, 12, 13, 14, 16, 17, 19, 27, 32, 33, 34, 36, 37, 41, 42, 45, 48, 50, 53, 60, 65, 66, 70, 72, 73, 78, 80, 82, 83, 87, 88, 91, 92, 93, 94, 96, 97, 108, 110, 111, 112, 113, 114, 115, 116, 117, 118, 119, 120, 122, 123, 127, 128, 130, 131, 132, 133, 134, 135, 136, 137, 138, 139, 140, 141, 143, 146, 147, 148, 149, 150, 152, 155, 157, 158, 160, 161, 162, 163, 164, 166, 167, 168, 169, 170, 171, 172, 174, 176
WALKER	8, 32, 33, 42, 43, 142, 157

Colorado blue columbine

Choke cherry blossoms

Nodding onion

If I stay here long enough

I will learn the art of silence.

When I have given up words

I will become what I have to say.

▲▲

Richard Shelton, poet

Mexican hat